D0869048

Colonial Williamsburg

hAUNTINGS

The Colonial Williamsburg Foundation
Williamsburg, Virginia

The Official Colonial Williamsburg Ghost Walk thanks Kelly Arehart, Leslie Bell-Stanton, Leigh Jameson, Bruce Luongo, Jennie McConnell, Michael Pfeifer, Melissa Winters, and all the writers and storytellers who have contributed to the program over the years.

25 24 23 22 21 20 19 18   3 4 5 6 7 8

Photography by Tom Green

Digital illustrations and design by Shanin Glenn

Library of Congress Cataloging-in-Publication Data

Names: Colonial Williamsburg Foundation.
Title: Colonial Williamsburg hauntings.
Description: Williamsburg, VA : Colonial Williamsburg Foundation, 2016.
Identifiers: LCCN 2016019827 | ISBN 9780879352844 (pbk. : alk. paper)
Subjects: LCSH: Haunted places–Virginia–Williamsburg.
Classification: LCC BF1472.U6 C65 2016 | DDC 133.109755/4252–dc23
LC record available at https://lccn.loc.gov/2016019827

The Colonial Williamsburg Foundation operates the world's largest living history museum—the restored eighteenth-century capital of Virginia.

Colonial Williamsburg® is a registered trade name of The Colonial Williamsburg Foundation.

The Colonial Williamsburg Foundation
PO Box 1776
Williamsburg, VA 23187-1776
colonialwilliamsburg.org

Printed in the United States of America

Contents

Foreword

Some might argue that the origins of this book date back to the eighteenth century. Certainly much of what you can see in the Historic Area of Colonial Williamsburg originated then, so perhaps the ghosts of the past still haunt us today. The more immediate basis for this book is the Official Colonial Williamsburg Ghost Walk, formerly known as the Tavern Ghost Walk, which was launched in 2004 to entertain guests as a supplemental Colonial Williamsburg tavern experience.

As the original name of the tour implies, the program initially focused on ghostly experiences of Colonial Williamsburg employees and guests at the four Historic Area dining taverns—Shields Tavern, King's Arms Tavern, Christiana Campbell's Tavern, and Chowning's Tavern. Over time, we collected more tales about the taverns and other historic sites.

The stories we tell on the tour come from guests, employees, and volunteers. Some of the ghostly experiences have even happened during a ghost walk. Who knows, maybe your story—should you be brave enough to retell the tale—will be the next one we weave into our program. Because the ghostly encounters took place in modern times, our tour guides are dressed in modern uniform and not—as with other Colonial Williamsburg programs—according to eighteenth-century fashion.

My own involvement with the program began in 2013 when I became the supervisor of the taverns' balladeers and character interpreters as well as the ghost walk. Since the summer of 2015, Leigh Jameson has been responsible for developing new stories and new locations so we can continue to expand the tour.

We continually grow, develop, and expand our tour. Thanks to the training, development, hard work, and great talents of our storytellers, the program becomes more popular every year. Even if you have taken our tour in years past, you will be delighted to return to hear new stories, visit new sites, and experience new twists and turns.

Each guide chooses the stories he or she loves to tell, so while there may be a few stories in common, no two tours are necessarily alike. We have woven into the stories bits of history from the eighteenth century to modern day to imagine the time and place when each ghost was still among the living.

This book chooses from among the stories you might hear on the tour and adds some history you won't hear on any of the tours. The book also features some illustrations of scenes that guests on the tour can only imagine.

This evening program is an all-outdoor walking tour even though the scenes described on the tour (and illustrated in the book) take place both indoors and outdoors. So join us as we wander the streets and gardens of Colonial Williamsburg's Historic Area, but beware of things that go bump in the night!

Kathryn Burnham—Hull
Tavern Program Supervisor
Evening Programs

Shields Tavern

A door unaccountably slams shut, chairs rearrange themselves, candles make their way back onto tables that had already been cleared, lights mysteriously turn on or off, disembodied voices are heard, shadows move through empty rooms. Staff and diners alike have experienced these bizarre happenings at Shields Tavern. In addition, some have sensed being followed or have heard footsteps precisely echoing their own as they walk through the tavern. Others have reported seeing in a mirror the reflection of a man in dark clothes standing on the stairs behind them in the lower room, but he is not on the stairs when they turn to look. In one case, while a couple was dining in the lower room, the wife felt the presence of someone sitting behind her on the staircase. She asked her husband, "He's behind me, isn't he?" Her husband silently nodded.

A "Lady in Green" also haunts the tavern. The Lady in Green is most frequently seen around a small corner room on the west side of the first floor, which was likely Mr. and Mrs. Shields's bedchamber. Cleaning up one evening, a server noticed a woman in a green colonial gown walking through the room. At first she thought it was a hostess, but hostesses do not wear green . . . or gowns. While cleaning up after lunch, another server looked up to see the lady in a corner. He was surprised to see her. She also gave a start, looked surprised, and "dissolved" right before his eyes.

An underground service tunnel links a freight elevator with Shields and the King's Arms Tavern. A hostess using the tunnel saw a woman in a stunning green dress walking toward her. The hostess returned a friendly wave before looking away briefly. When she looked back, the Lady in Green was gone—mysterious indeed as the tunnel itself is twenty yards long with no other exits, and neither of the kitchen staffs had seen her.

11

A waitress looked in the

mirror and saw a lady in

a green gown.

The Lady in Green has also been seen in the lower room where a waitress glanced in a mirror and, instead of seeing herself, saw a lady in a gorgeous green gown. When the waitress stepped back for another look in the mirror, she saw just herself. Other employees have seen the lady "looking lost" just outside the pantry.

One evening brought more excitement than usual to the tavern. Portraits of the Roman emperors line the walls of the front hall where diners wait to be seated. While a particularly rowdy school group was being led to their dining room, with the children shouting and joking loudly, the pictures began to shake. A hush fell over the group as they watched. Then the pictures began to pop off the walls, one by one, falling to the floor with thunderous crashes. Not one, however, had broken—not even a crack in the glass. Perhaps that evening the ghosts of the tavern just wanted some peace and quiet.

At least two individuals from the eighteenth century might have reason to haunt Shields Tavern: Jean Marot and his step-granddaughter Frances Shields, both of whose lives appear to have come to untimely ends.

A French Huguenot, Jean Marot, known as John, came to Virginia to escape persecution in Catholic France. He arrived in Virginia in 1700, and for four to five years he was a servant to a planter named William Byrd. Marot was living in Williamsburg in 1705 when he got his first tavern license, but where that tavern was is unknown. In January 1708, Marot bought the lot near the Capitol with a building on it, finishing his first addition to it probably in 1708, and likely began keeping a tavern there that year. A booming business allowed Marot to expand the tavern over the next ten years. But tragedy struck in the fall of 1717 when he died under mysterious circumstances.

Francis Sharpe was indicted for the murder of John Marot and stood trial at the Capitol. Marot's actual date of death is unknown, but it was probably close to November 18, 1717, when the York County court heard evidence against Sharpe, convincing them that he should be tried for murder. The records of the General Court for 1717 have been lost to time, but Sharpe must have been cleared of the murder charge since records from 1718 indicate that he got a tavern license that May. The existing records do not elaborate on the circumstances.

15

Was Sharpe truly innocent or was something more devious at play? If Sharpe did kill Marot, did he do so accidentally or with intent? Was he killed instantly or was he wounded and later died from the wounds?

John Marot's daughter Anne, same name as her mother, married James Shields around 1738, and they took over the proprietorship of the tavern by 1745, when they bought it from Anne's sister and her husband, Edith and Samuel Cobbs. With eighteen dining tables, fourteen fully outfitted beds, and backgammon and billiards for entertainment, it became popular with the middling sort. Anne and James Shields, both of whom had been widowed with one and three daughters respectively, probably lived in the tavern with the four girls and the three children they had together. But James's daughter Frances, born between 1730 and 1732, appears to have passed away as a girl or a young woman because she is the only child of Shields not mentioned in his updated will of 1747.

Did John Marot and Frances Shields stay in the tavern after their deaths? Or did they return at some point? Are there others with them?

John Marot and Francis Sharpe—Business Rivals?

John Marot and Francis Sharpe were both tavern keepers. Though it is not clear where Sharpe's business was located since he owned several lots in Williamsburg, he did own lots directly across the street from Marot. Since Sharpe also had a tavern license by 1718, he likely owned a tavern somewhere. It may well have been across from Marot's since those lots continued to house a tavern for many years after Sharpe left Williamsburg. Was there perhaps some kind of business rivalry that led to Marot's death, or at least the indictment of Sharpe for the murder?

What Became of John Marot's Widow?

The widow Marot remarried quickly—perhaps too quickly for the soul of her recently departed spouse. Her new husband, Timothy Sullivant, took out a tavern license in the spring of 1718, but he turned the business over to his wife by 1721. No doubt Sullivant enjoyed the substantial estate left by John Marot in light of the fact that when Sullivant died in 1730, his own estate was worth very little—perhaps another thorn to keep Marot from resting in peace. Widowed again, Anne Marot Sullivant may have turned the tavern into a boardinghouse. She left Williamsburg for Amelia County in 1738, moving in with her daughter Edith and son-in-law Samuel Cobbs. She died in 1742.

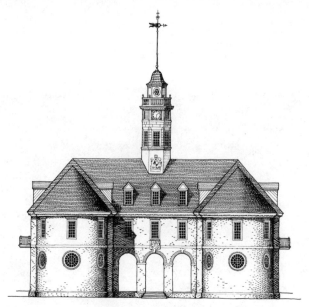

Capitol

After fire destroyed the Jamestown statehouse for the third time in 1698, the burgesses decided to move the colony's government to Middle Plantation, soon renamed Williamsburg. On June 6, 1699, they resolved to build what became the first American structure to which the word "Capitol" was applied. To blunt the threat of fire, this new building was constructed without fireplaces. Candles and smoking were barred. But in 1723, the secretary complained that the building was damp, so fireplaces were added to help keep the Capitol dry. As had been feared, a fire started in the early hours of January 30, 1747. It left only some walls and the foundation. A second Capitol was built by 1753, but in 1780 the General Assembly moved to Richmond. The west wing was demolished and its bricks sold in 1793; the east burned in 1832. The history of fire seems to burn on.

Early one morning, Colonial Williamsburg's Security and Safety office received an alert that a fire alarm was going off in the reconstructed Capitol. Scrambling to prevent a third instance of the building being gutted by flames, officers hurried to the site. Though they saw no flames or even smoke, they ran through the building throwing open every door to check for fire and people who might have become trapped. The search of the first and second floors produced nothing. On the third floor, the officers found a locked door that neither had the key to open. One officer headed back to the cruiser for an additional set of keys to the building, but, upon hearing a door slam on the second floor, quickly rechecked the rooms on the second floor, calling out "Security!" as he went. He again found the building empty.

After retrieving the other set of keys, the officers again tried the locked door. While struggling with the lock, they heard the loud slam of a door again on the floor below,

19

Security officers had

no key for this door.

but they found nothing. Security was never able to deter-mine why the fire alarm went off, but some think these false alarms are a part of the property's own memory.

Despite the burnings, the Capitol did see many useful and productive years as a government building. It hosted soaring speeches and heated debates as the country drew closer and closer to Revolution. Today, the reconstructed building honors these moments and also hosts an evening program reenacting the trial of Grace Sherwood, who was tried for witchcraft in 1706.

Sherwood lived in Pungo, a small community outside of what is now Virginia Beach. Married to a small landowner, James Sherwood, she was a midwife and a healer who used herbs to heal people and animals. In 1697 Sher-wood's troubles began when Richard Capps, another local farmer, accused her of using sorcery to kill one of his bulls. The case was ultimately dismissed, but it planted seeds of suspicion about Sherwood throughout the community that would persist. In 1698, John Gisburne accused her of bewitching his pigs and cotton. Another accused her of intruding into homes and escaping through the keyhole in the shape of a black cat.

Circumstances came to a head in 1705 when Sherwood was involved in a physical altercation with Elizabeth Hill. Sherwood sued Hill for assault and battery and was awarded twenty shillings sterling. Perhaps out of revenge, Hill and her husband accused Sherwood of witchcraft. She was brought before the county court, which ordered a jury of five women to inspect her body for suspicious or unusual markings that would suggest dealings with the devil. The women found two dark, raised marks and "Severall other Spotts."

23

The case eventually proceeded to trial by ducking. Sherwood was taken out in a boat and thrown into the water. If she floated, it was evidence that she was a witch. Sherwood quickly emerged at the surface, perhaps floating, perhaps swimming, perhaps some combination, but apparently enough to convince a jury of women to search her again. The women "Declared on Oath that She is not like them nor noe Other women that they know of, having two things . . . on her private parts of a Black Coller [color] being Blacker than the Rest of her Body." The county court found that the results of the ducking and the search were enough to continue with trial. The court records of the

Did the ghost of Grace
Sherwood come back to
watch reenactments of
her trial for witchcraft?

proceedings were lost in a fire, but had Sherwood been found guilty, she would have been executed, and since she appears again in the Princess Anne County Court records in 1708, she was not. Her will was recorded in Princess Anne County on October 1, 1740.

Today, Colonial Williamsburg's guests can relive Sherwood's trial and decide her guilt or innocence inside the Capitol. Many of the interpreters who participate in "Cry Witch!" and also members of the audience have reported seeing a woman watching the proceedings from the galleries above the courtroom. She is always described the same way: plain dark clothes of the early eighteenth century, a white apron, and a white cap set over dirty blonde hair that has fallen loose. These balconies are not for public use, and no employees use the galleries during the performance. Has Sherwood's ghost come to rest in the Capitol? Maybe this spectator is obsessed with the injustice done to her by a fearful community? Or perhaps she hopes to be vindicated as modern visitors ask questions of the witnesses, weigh the evidence, and determine her guilt or innocence.

Virginians Skeptical of Witchcraft?

Massachusetts villagers may have been quick to condemn people who were accused of witchcraft in Salem, but, at least in the case of Grace Sherwood, early Virginians seemed much more hesitant. First, the case was shuffled around in the courts. The initial verdict of the county court resulted in the removal of Sherwood's case to the Council of Virginia, which referred it to the attorney general. The attorney general said the "charge or accusation is too general" and sent the case back to the county court. Then the county court appointed another jury of women to inspect Sherwood again, but the women declined to appear in court. They weren't scared to examine her, so were they perhaps unwilling to support the accusation? Two months went by (a long time for the colonial legal system) before the court settled on ducking. Before she was taken out in the boat, a group of women was to "Shift & Serch her before She goe into the water that She Carry nothing about her to cause any further Suspicion." So that she could be condemned or cleared? Either way, a very sensible move. The court seems to have been concerned that she not drown, almost expecting her not to be able to save herself because she was not a witch: "Take the said Grace forthwith & put her into above mans Debth & try her how she Swims therein having Care of her life to preserve her from Drowning." In fact, the first date settled for her ducking was "very Rainy & Bad Soe that possibly might endanger her health," so they rescheduled.

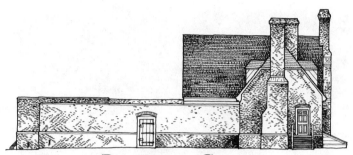

Public Gaol

Unheated, overcrowded, dirty cells, a place of discomfort and pestilence where "gaol fever"—probably typhus—and smallpox broke out from time to time, these miserable chambers played host to an extensive cast of characters after they opened in 1703 or 1704. Most occupants were short-term, men and women awaiting trial or convicts waiting to be branded, whipped, or hanged. (Punishment was swift, and though sentences were harsh by modern standards, first offenders might expect mercy, and some miscreants were merely fined.) Occasionally people with mental health disorders were confined in the gaol, and during the Revolution, Tories, spies, military prisoners, deserters, and traitors were included in the prisoner inventory.

One prisoner had a longer than normal stay. In October 1764, Abigail Briggs, described as an "Indian woman" and a servant but not whether she was free or enslaved, was put on trial for the murder of a "negro" man, probably enslaved, on the plantation where they worked. Despite the testimony that she was always a quiet woman and the deceased an angry man, it is clear that Briggs hit the man with a kitchen implement: "she took . . . up as the first Thing she could lay her hands on, to defend herself against the Assault of her fellow Servant." His head hit the stone floor.

29

She was examined in her county court and brought to Williamsburg to trial. In April 1765 she was found guilty of murder and sentenced to hang. The governor, who believed Briggs was defending herself, took interest in the proceedings and felt the evidence would support a lesser charge of manslaughter, which could be pardoned. He went so far as to state that "had she been a white woman," she would have been found guilty of manslaughter only. The governor petitioned for a royal pardon in August. Eventually it was granted, and Abigail Briggs was released around March 1766. She had spent nearly a year and a half imprisoned.

Charged with murder,

Abigail Briggs spent

a year and a half in

the gaol.

Perhaps the most famous occupants were pirates—fifteen of Blackbeard's accomplices who were brought to Williamsburg to stand trial after Blackbeard himself had been vanquished by Lt. Robert Maynard of the Royal Navy. One of the henchmen was acquitted, one was pardoned, and the rest were sentenced to hang.

Another notorious inmate was the British lieutenant governor Henry Hamilton, considered by many Virginians to be more of a war criminal than a mere prisoner of war. The "Hair-Buyer General," who was captured at Vincennes, in what is now Indiana, reportedly paid bounties to American Indians who brought him the scalps of those fighting for American independence.

What more likely place for spirits to haunt?

One warm day, one of the site interpreters was opening up the doors of the Gaol to allow the breeze to come in. As he walked from the back door to the parlor room, he heard what sounded like a coin dropping behind him. He turned and found a penny on the floor. He bent down to pick it up and then heard the sound behind him again. He turned to find another penny on the floor. He bent to pick it up, and again he heard the noise. It sounded like the coins were falling from the ceiling, so he looked up to see if someone was playing a joke on him but found that there was no way to drop anything from above. Pennies continued to drop periodically for nearly five more minutes until the interpreter announced to the otherwise empty room: "Mr. Pelham, if you insist on throwing money, make it shillings, pounds, or even twenties!" The pennies stopped dropping, and the interpreter found himself thirty-five cents richer.

The interpreter was appealing to Peter Pelham, the last traditional gaolkeeper, from 1771–1779. To maintain his somewhat large family—Pelham and his wife, Ann, had fourteen children—Pelham held numerous jobs, including organist at Bruton Parish Church. It appears that Pelham was more successful as an organist than as a gaoler, enjoying his job as organist for over forty years but being investigated (though cleared) for the number of prisoners who escaped under his watch.

Another time, an officer patrolling the area after dark saw a light in the building although it had been closed some time earlier. The officer found the door unlocked but no one inside. After turning out the light and locking the door, he went on his way. About an hour later, he saw a

Coins fell from the

ceiling, but there was

no one above.

Was the gaol unlocked

by the ghost of a former

gaoler with a reputation

for forgetting to lock up?

light once more. Again, the door was wide open and no-body present. All in all, the Gaol apparently unlocked itself four times that night—well into the early morning hours. Although possible, it is very unlikely that anyone entrusted with a key would have repeatedly opened the building and left it unattended throughout the night. Unless, of course, that person happened to be the ghost of a former gaoler with a reputation for forgetting to lock up.

If Pelham is haunting the premises, he is not alone. Another site interpreter was closing up the outdoor cells one evening and felt the strange sensation that someone was be-hind him. He turned to find an empty courtyard, but glancing up he saw behind the windows of the upper cells the source of the sensation—a woman with a round, dirty face and stringy black hair peering down at him. Puzzled he walked up the steps toward her. She backed into the shadows, and when he opened the door, the room was empty. Could she have been one of the indentured servants housed in the gaol for murder? Or perhaps someone with mental illness that called the gaol home before the Public Hospital was opened in 1773? Or might she have been Abigail Briggs?

The Pelham Family—Not As Large As It Sounds

Peter Pelham and his wife, Ann, did have fourteen children, but four of the children, Thomas, Lucy I, Ann II, and Mary, died as infants and another two, Ann I and Lucy II, died before age five. Peter and Charles, the eldest two, had reached their majority and were likely out of the house by the time Pelham became gaoler, and Sarah married about 1773. When Pelham became gaoler, therefore, there were likely only five children living at home, and the same after Sarah's marriage, as the youngest, Parthenia, was born in 1772. This was not an uncommon number of dependents to provide for in the eighteenth century, and Pelham had income not only from the gaol and the church but also from music lessons, his work as a clerk to two governors and as committee clerk in the House of Burgesses, and a limited amount of mercantile activity.

King's Arms Tavern

Not all of the ghosts in Colonial Williamsburg's Historic Area are colonial. The King's Arms Tavern is a case in point. Opened by Jane Vobe in 1772, the King's Arms was one of the finest establishments in Williamsburg. It catered to Virginia's gentry and the politically influential before, during, and after the Revolution.

Today's King's Arms, originally reconstructed in the early 1950s to include the Alexander Purdie House to increase its size, started serving guests again in 1951. One of the tavern's employees from that early period was a spunky assistant manager named Erna. From all accounts, Erna was a competent supervisor and enjoyed her job. Unfortunately, she passed away unexpectedly. She not only had worked at the tavern but also had lived in an apartment over the Purdie half. Ever since, guests and employees have fallen into the habit of affectionately attributing inexplicable happenings to her. "Erna" is sometimes playful and sometimes a bit vindictive.

One waiter recounts setting up a dinner station in an upstairs room one evening, stacking four or five bread plates on the inside ledge of an open window. When he turned around, his plates were gone. Puzzled, he looked out the window and saw the plates comfortably sitting on the ground two stories below as if they had been placed there. None were broken or even chipped. Might this have been evidence of Erna's mischievousness?

Was it Erna helping out or fooling around one night when the manager and an employee had closed up but, on leaving, noticed a window open—one that was never opened because it was in a staircase and too hard to get to. The manager went for a ladder, but on his return he found the hostess wide-eyed and pale. The window had slowly closed and latched itself as she watched.

Guests may notice how the employees at the King's

Plates mysteriously

reappeared two stories

below where the waiter

had left them.

Arms go out of their way to stay on Erna's good side. When they arrive, they say, "Good morning, Erna," and when they leave, they similarly wish her a good night. What motivates these polite rituals?

It's said that Erna has a habit of pushing or tripping those who annoy her. A new hire recalled sweeping the front steps and, out of nowhere, feeling as if two hands had pushed her down the stairs. Seeing no one around, she ran into the building in hysterics. Her fellow staff members filled her in on Erna.

44

Employees of the tavern are not the only people Erna targets. Just after one tour group that included a group of servicemen left the tavern, their guide heard a loud thud behind her. She turned to see one of the soldiers on the ground with no one else near him. He delightedly shared that something had just pushed him down, thrilled to hear that it might have been Erna's doing.

Perhaps it is some other spirit or spirits that haunt the King's Arms, but skeptics of any stripe beware: even just thinking ill of Erna has produced bad results. One hot July evening, a ghost tour guide found herself sweaty and exhausted, ready to go home for the night. Passing the

King's Arms Tavern, she began silently thinking that directing her guests to say good night to Erna was a stupid and tired superstition. Moments later, she found herself, dazed and confused, lying face down in the middle of Duke of Gloucester Street.

Let their misfortunes guide your own safe travels through Williamsburg—if you find yourself at the King's Arms, make sure you say good night to Erna.

45

Alexander Purdie House

Reconstructed and today part of the King's Arms Tavern, the Alexander Purdie House is named after the man who purchased it in 1767, but its ghosts come from the Civil War era. By 1835 Richard M. Bucktrout owned the house. Bucktrout Funeral Service of Williamsburg is the oldest funeral business in the country, operating since 1759. The Purdie House was the site of that business for some time in the 1800s. Richard's feisty daughter Delia inherited the business from her father when he died just after the war. In 1862, when Delia was just fifteen, as the Union army marched down Duke of Gloucester Street, Delia is said to have stood on her front porch and spat on the

Undertaker Richard Bucktrout
and His Creepy Daybook

From 1850 to 1866, Richard Manning Bucktrout, a
merchant, undertaker, and carpenter, kept a daybook
of his many business dealings. Although it is largely
a mundane list of sales, deliveries, repairs, and
account information, many of the funeral records are
surprisingly detailed, and occasionally graphic. Funeral
records increase especially around the time of the Civil
War Battle of Williamsburg. Entries sometimes include
information on where and how the person died and often
where the body was buried or sent. According to an entry
for February 26, 1859, Pleasant Baker, for example,
"cut his throat with a raisor on friday morning about
1/2 an hour by sunrise in the woods behind my house in
the soldiers grave yard." About a week later, Benjamin
Handsford "cut his throat with a razor also . . . with
a handkerchief tied around the handle . . . to keep it
from giving way." An odd entry for December 7, 1861,
lists a coffin for Jasper Clemons, of the Tenth Georgia
Regiment, who "is packed up at my house now." "Captn
Librock" was "one of the Soldiers that got drowned."
Numerous entries refer to coffins for children.
Especially sad are those that refer to more than
one child in a household. Such was the case for
a Mr. Lyons: "2 very fine coffins for 2 of your
children died in 2 or 3 days of each other."

soldiers as they marched past. By the close of the war, she had been serving as a spy and mail runner (she is said to have hidden mail and other communications in her hoop skirt) between Williamsburg and Richmond. She married and settled down with William Henry Braithwaite, a former Confederate soldier, and took over the family business. She ran it until 1908, though she probably moved it at some point to another location.

The Purdie House has been described as having a certain "energy" or "presence." Hardly surprising given its history. Guests and employees alike have experienced cold spots and unexplained noises. A tavern worker described a chilled hand pressed through her clothes and against her stomach. More chilling, knowing of Delia and her feisty personality, are the frequent sightings of a Civil War couple in various parts of town. A gentleman in a Confederate uniform and a lady in a broad, bell-shaped gown have been seen strolling on Francis Street near the King's Arms Tavern parking lot and where Delia and her husband had their family home. They have also been seen on Duke of Gloucester Street in the area of the Purdie House. A security officer making his rounds in the early morning hours driving down Duke of Gloucester Street spotted two Civil War people that looked to be "dressed for a fancy ball." He doubled back to see them again, but they had vanished.

Perhaps the continuing presence of ghosts from the Civil War can be attributed to Williamsburg's Civil War history. Did some of those who died in battle never leave the area? And might some of the townspeople have been so bitter about the occupation that followed the battle that they refused to leave the town to the Yankees—even after they died?

Civil War as well as

Revolutionary War

ghosts may haunt the

streets of Williamsburg.

The Civil War in Williamsburg

The Battle of Williamsburg on May 5, 1862, was long and bloody. It resulted from Union troops pushing up the Peninsula from Fort Monroe in Hampton Roads as part of an attempt to take Richmond, the Confederate capital. The Confederate army had established defensive positions in Yorktown and Williamsburg. After holding Union troops at Yorktown for about a month, the Confederate forces fell back to Williamsburg with the Union forces in pursuit. Much of the Confederate army continued marching to Richmond. Those that were left to delay the Union troops fought all day in driving rain. In addition, several units turned back to Williamsburg to help as the battle intensified. According to the official report of Union general Joseph Hooker, the battle swelled to "one of gigantic proportions." With the rain and the cramped, swampy terrain with its tangled vegetation, it was a close, messy, confusing battle. Soldiers were exhausted and running low on ammunition, though fresh brigades arrived periodically throughout the day on each side. Williamsburg's buildings, both private and public, overflowed with the casualties. It wasn't until late in the day that Union forces finally outmaneuvered and overpowered the Confederates, and what was left of the Confederate army abandoned Williamsburg. The combat lasted ten hours and resulted in four thousand dead, wounded, and captured.

Prentis Store

Most of the ghosts of Williamsburg are harmless—mysterious appearances, unexpected noises, eerie sensations. One strange happening at the Prentis Store, however, was more harrowing.

One slow winter's day, just one employee and two female guests occupied the store. The two women were standing near the center of the store, one on each side of a barrel containing heavy gate weights. The salesperson was nearby. On a shelf behind the sales counter, a large checkerboard was displayed behind a pyramid of three pottery mugs. As the women browsed the merchandise, one of them made a negative comment about the upkeep of the store. Suddenly, the checkerboard came flying across the room, striking the barrel between the two women and shattering into pieces. The mugs stacked in front of the board had not been disturbed at all. The employee quickly ushered the women into the street, closing up shop until his manager returned.

Another game board was mounted on the wall where the former had been, but this time the staff secured it with two small iron brackets to ensure it wouldn't be flying around the store anytime soon. If only it had been that easy.

55

An employee having a particularly rough day on the job was standing at her register about three or four feet away from the shelf with the checkerboard when she did what many people do when things are not going well at work: she muttered a disparaging remark about her place of business. The checkerboard, she said, "hopped off the wall" and struck her on the side of the head! Fortunately she was not seriously hurt.

Buyers beware—the firm of William Prentis and Company operated a highly successful store from 1733 until the Revolution in this original building, and it seems to be haunted by particularly prideful spirits. Ghostly guardians

Checkers can be a

dangerous game . . .

when ghosts are around.

of the shop's proud heritage appear to bring woe to those who speak ill of the establishment or its fine goods. Perhaps because of their pride in the store, the Prentis ghosts seem unable to take a break from their work. The sounds of someone counting coins upstairs and boxes of merchandise being moved in the basement have been heard on several occasions when no one was in those rooms.

But one ghost seems unrelated to the store: An employee once felt a cold hand on her shoulder when she was in the basement. Turning, she briefly saw a man dressed in a Confederate uniform. He quickly vanished, but the employee has firmly refused to ever go into the basement again. Perhaps the soldier was one who died during the Civil War Battle of Williamsburg.

If you find yourself shopping at the Prentis Store, stay out of the basement, be sure to keep one eye on the checkerboards, and mind your manners—Mr. Prentis and his staff may not respond consistently, but you may be the unlucky one to whom he does respond.

William Prentis—From Pauper to Proprietor

William Prentis was born in London in October 1699, one of five children. When his mother died in 1707, his struggling father, a baker working as a porter, enrolled him in Christ's Hospital, which was founded in 1552 by the king for the education of poor children. At age fifteen, Prentis was apprenticed and sailed over the Atlantic to work for Archibald Blair of Williamsburg. Prentis's charitable education, and probably a sharp mind and hard-working nature, must have served him well because when Blair died in 1733, Prentis was managing the store that Blair and his partner owned. Blair had left his half share in the store in equal amounts to his three daughters, and Prentis had saved enough money to purchase one of those shares. Thus he owned one-sixth of the store. The name of the store was soon changed to William Prentis and Company, and Prentis's impressive business acumen grew the business considerably. He became one of the most successful men in Williamsburg.

A ghost's hand on

your shoulder is sure

to cause a shiver.

Brick House Tavern

Today the Brick House Tavern is a hotel facility, one of Colonial Williamsburg's Colonial Houses–Historic Lodging. Located on Duke of Gloucester Street, it has sixteen rooms, eight on each floor. There is a great room with a fireplace in the basement. Guests who have stayed in the Brick House Tavern typically encounter nothing remarkable, but a few stories might raise a few eyebrows—or hairs.

Two sisters, who had visited before, stayed at the Brick House Tavern on the second floor. The first night in the tavern after they turned out the lights around midnight, a shadow passed along the wall across from the dormer windows, which seemed odd because a true shadow could have been cast there only by someone walking on the gabled roof. Around two in the morning, the sound of jingling keys aroused one of the sisters. The sound was coming from the center of the room. It continued for twenty minutes, though the guest couldn't see anything making the noise. The other sister was awakened the following night by something or someone kicking or bumping her bed. The thumping moved from the bottom of the bed to the top. When it reached the area where the pillow was, she felt a heaviness as if someone was sitting on her chest. Her yell of "Help!" awakened her sister, and the heaviness stopped. She dashed to the bathroom to turn on the light. A "small smoky mist" trailed across the ceiling and disappeared as if it went through the wall. On the third night, they left the closet light on and had no unusual experiences. During the first three days of their stay, they also noticed at times a strong, pleasant sweet tobacco scent on the stairs and landing. Smoking, however, is prohibited in the building, and, very strangely, the sisters noticed that there was no trace of the scent if they returned to the spot where they first smelled it—even if they returned immediately.

On another occasion, a couple of guests were asleep,

How could there be

a shadow but no figure

to cast it?

also on the second floor, when a sound woke them up in the middle of the night. The sound was coming through the wall behind the headboards. It sounded as if someone wearing boots was in the next room walking across a wooden floor. The sound then passed into their room, though there was no door in that wall. They could hear the sound of boots on a bare wooden floor walking across their room. But the room was carpeted. The boot steps went out the door and down the stairs. Then they heard the entrance door open and close.

66

Another time, a housekeeper finished cleaning a room. From the hallway just outside it, she saw a man in a "puffy-sleeved" shirt standing in the room. He hadn't been there the moment before and was gone by the time she looked more carefully. It was the same room the two guests had stayed in. One of the guests, a frequent visitor, returned and stayed in the room across the hall. Once again she awoke in the middle of the night to the sound of boot steps going down the stairs.

Yet another time, a guest was awakened about one or two o'clock in the morning by rustling near her head. She opened her eyes and looked directly up into the ghostly face of a man dressed in a blue-checkered shirt and a three-cornered hat. The guest started to sit up in bed and called to her roommate. As the roommate turned on the bedside light, the ghost disappeared as a "wispy trail of smoke" across the ceiling and through the wall.

Identifying this spirit, or these spirits, is pretty near impossible. The building has had numerous owners and the tavern many tenants. The earliest known owner of the lot was Thomas Ravenscroft, who conveyed the property in 1723 to Cole Digges. There were buildings on it at the time. Subsequent owners included Dudley Digges and William Withers, who in 1760 conveyed a small strip to William Holt and the remaining part in 1761 to William Carter, a physician. Dr. Carter appears to have built this two-story building as a multiunit rental property in the early 1760s. By March 1770, Mary Davis was established at "Dr. Carter's large brick house," where she had opened a lodging house. She advertised "12 or 14 very good lodging rooms" and also noted that the first-floor rooms were reserved for ladies and the rooms above for gentlemen. Itinerant tradesmen and others with services or goods to sell would arrange for lodging here, advertise in the *Virginia*

She opened her eyes and

looked directly up into

the ghostly face with a

three-cornered hat.

Gazette, and show their wares to customers in their rooms. If business seemed promising, they might settle down else-where in town; if not, they would move on. Over time, a surgeon, a jeweler, a watch repairer, a milliner, a wig-maker, and several tavern keepers, to name a few, called the Brick House Tavern home. Any of these, at least those who were male, could be our ghost or ghosts.

Peyton Randolph House

Strange shadows. Slamming doors. Pressing feelings. Odd knocks and noises. The Peyton Randolph House is among the most haunted houses in America. The home of one of the most prominent families in colonial Virginia, the deep-red Peyton Randolph House is one of the oldest and most historic buildings in Williamsburg. The house has three sections, with the original section of the structure built in 1715. The three centuries of history associated with this home have produced an unusually large number of ghostly tales.

Why is this such an active building? One theory involves the Peachey family who owned the house during the first half of the nineteenth century. After the ownership of the property passed out of the Randolph family, the Peacheys took up residence. T. G. Peachey was a planter. His mother was a Cary and a Blair, and therefore they were related to various Virginians of note in the area. According to the family Bible, he was buried in a family graveyard in the garden of the house, the exact placement of which is unknown. Peachey's daughter Sally died in September 1839 at age two, and his daughter Mary died before she was ten, possibly at age eight at or around the same time as her sister. Many have suggested that perhaps the children did not go far.

Security staff check the buildings regularly every night. In the small hours of the morning, an officer was running his second check through the house. He always worked west to east on the lower floor, then the upper floor east to west, then the basement. This particular night, he entered the building, relocked the door behind him, and started to move through when he heard footsteps above him. He stopped and called out. No reply. He continued his check. As he was climbing the stairs to the upper rooms, he heard a faint knock on the front door. He went back down and

73

called out. No reply. Back up the stairs reversing path east to west. All clear. He went down the back stairs and paused. He had heard the giggles of children from the upper rooms. Then he heard what sounded like a ball drop and roll across the ceiling above him and the pitter-patter of little feet chasing after it. Knowing there was no one in those rooms, he quickly made his exit.

But the story of the Peachey children doesn't end there. Several years ago, as a group was leaving this site and heading for the next, a young girl of eleven or twelve asked the guide if there were any supernatural stories about children in the house. At the time, the tour guides had nothing specific, and the guide told her no. When the tour was over, the girl and her mother approached again. The mother explained that her daughter had inquired because she had seen a young child looking out of the window on the top right of the house. About two weeks later, a boy of around the same age asked the same question for the same reason—a young child had been looking out of the window on the top right of the house. The location would put the apparition in a spot that corresponded to someone dropping the ball that the security guard had heard.

Unfortunately, not all the residents of the building have been as playful, and not all the shadows are friendly. Another time when a security guard was on his nightly check, he entered the house, worked the lower floor, then upper floor, and then walked down to the basement. Since there are no modern lights in the building, the guards use flashlights. When he reached the bottom of the steps, the door to the basement swung shut. He also heard it lock. Slightly irritated, he turned toward the stairs and swept the flashlight towards the door when the battery died. As he started to feel his way over, something grabbed him around his lower legs. He froze. He could not slide his feet. He could not pick up his legs. He could not move. Something had him. Terrified, he reached for his walkie-talkie and called in to the dispatch. When backup arrived, they entered the house and found the basement door locked. They called to the officer in the basement and heard him respond, saying he couldn't move. When they pounded on the basement door, the lock released and so did the hold on the officer. He never spoke of those long minutes in that basement. He refused to return to the Randolph House alone. He left the job by the end of the month.

Though the house was

locked, some heard

the sounds of children

playing . . .

. . . and others saw

a young child looking

out the window.

Perhaps this shadow remains from Richard Hansford, the owner of the house from just before the Civil War to the 1880s. He lived a life fraught with vile deeds and shady connections. He was a slave trader. He made his living on lives—buying and selling, splitting apart loved ones and devastating families. He also served as director of the Public Hospital, where his brother Charles was treasurer during a period of known misappropriations of funds: Charles was writing himself checks from the hospital's accounts—taking money from people who were poor and mentally ill. What kind of spirit might such a man as Richard—or Charles for that matter—leave behind?

Chowning's Tavern

Chowning's Tavern, built around 1750, was advertised in 1766 to serve "all who please to favour [Mr. Chowning] with their custom," in other words, the common man. The building has seen its share of apparitions: a man dressed in colonial clothing in a mirror but not in the room, the reflection of the face of a woman in a green hood in an upstairs window, an indistinct misty form the height and shape of a person, a little blonde girl in colonial clothing sitting at a table who appeared and disappeared within seconds, a man in colonial garb who walked across the upstairs dining room and through the wall.

A balladeer was standing in the doorway of the dividing wall in the barroom. Feeling a hand on his shoulder that he assumed was a waiter's, he moved to allow the waiter to pass easily. However, as he looked back as he stepped aside, he saw no one there.

As a waitress paused at her serving station and was surveying her tables, she suddenly felt something grab the shoulders of her dress and pull upward. Several guests also saw the short gown raise up a few inches with no apparent help.

The chairs in this tavern seem to have working legs. As several employees chatted in the barroom after work, someone noticed a chair out of place across the room, despite the fact that all had been in order moments before. They set the chair back at the table, but a few minutes later it was back across the room, apparently of its own accord. Another time, another group of four employees were sitting at a table after work. One got up for a soda. When she returned, her chair was halfway across the room—without anyone noticing. A summer employee liked to take his lunch in the quiet upstairs dining room—that is, he did until he saw a chair move from one end of the room to the other. Another time, while three employees were sitting in that

83

A little girl in colonial

clothing appeared and

disappeared.

same room chatting, one of their chairs, with the employee in it, started to move—backwards, sideways, and then a half-turn. Tables too. Two tables that one server tried to put together for a large group refused to stay together. Every time the server put them together, they moved slowly apart as the server watched. None of these employees were particularly amused.

One day a guest who was not easily spooked came down from the upstairs dining room to chat with the staff. She said she had spoken with the ghost of a colonial man named Peter who sat staring out the back window at the place where his house used to be. He said he was fond of one of the hostesses and wanted to be a protector of her and her son who was born early. The hostess was surprised that the guest would know of her son. She wasn't convinced, though, and responded that she didn't believe in ghosts. The guest then said that Peter had left her a white flower the day before. This shocked the hostess because the previous day, after she had seated some guests in the garden, she had stepped back to find a magnolia blossom at her feet. Although magnolias are common, the closest tree was a block away, and the blossoms are large and heavy for a flower—not something that could have just blown there.

Did the ghost of a

colonial man leave a

magnolia blossom for

a tavern hostess?

Market Square Tavern

Market Square Tavern is a hotel facility today, one of Colonial Williamsburg's Colonial Houses—Historic Lodging. Located on Duke of Gloucester Street next to Market Square, it has six rooms on the first floor and five on the second. There is a great room with a fireplace on the first floor.

A few years ago, a group of about fifteen rented the entire Market Square Tavern for their lodging. On their first night, several of them were sitting in the great room, on the first floor. After a while, they realized they had been hearing the sound of someone pacing in the hallway. The sound continued for some time, and they naturally were curious as to who of their group was pacing for so long and why.

One of the men went to check. There was no one there, but the hallway was curiously cold. Knowing that the building was an original and that Thomas Jefferson had stayed there while studying law with George Wythe, the group jokingly referred to their mysterious pacer as "Tom." Later that night, after everyone had gone to bed, the same gentleman went back into the living room to retrieve a book. He jokingly said, "Good night, Tom." As he did, he heard the small sound of a chair scraping slightly as if someone had stood up. Looking around, he saw that the Windsor chair by the window was slightly cocked and that the curtain was moving gently. The next morning, one of the group whose room was off the first-floor hallway and who had not sat up the previous night asked who had been stomping around the hall the night before. The noise had kept him awake.

The specter might well have been the shade of Thomas Jefferson, but it could also have been any number of other people. A store was first built on this lot in 1750 or 1751. The structure was enlarged and remodeled various times during the eighteenth century and after, and a store, tavern, or public house has been on this lot ever since, so a lot of people have come through its doors.

Streets

During an early morning walk, one visiting couple encountered another couple dressed in colonial garb. They spoke for a bit, the visiting couple thinking how charming it was that the couple remained in character using eighteenth-century speech and mannerisms. They wished each other a good day and parted, but very quickly the visiting couple turned back to the colonial couple with an additional query. The street was empty in all directions.

Bus

One rainy summer evening, a shuttle bus with a handful of passengers pulled into the Merchants Square stop. No one was waiting, but the driver decided to linger a few minutes so as not to leave any guests waiting in the bad weather. Suddenly the doors were forced open, and footprints, as if left by wet shoes, appeared on the steps. No one appeared to be there. The driver and passengers watched, terrified, as the footprints "walked" down the length of the bus. In December of that year, the bus driver reported that the bus he was driving that night had been in the shop more than it had been on the streets since that August evening. He suggested that "whatever got on that bus that night never got off."

Some Final Thoughts

Despite the challenges issued by the spirits colonial and otherwise, Colonial Williamsburg employees will not be thwarted in the mission with which they are entrusted: to preserve the Historic Area and provide for guests' needs so that the future may learn from the past.

When an employee was closing up Shields Tavern one night when Hurricane Isabel was on the way, one of the windows kept reopening by itself as if an unseen hand were pushing it up. The employee finally went and got a hammer and nailed the window shut. When the manager, having seen her put away the hammer, asked her what was up, she told her story. The manager commented that it was probably just the spooks of the tavern playing tricks on her.

The employee responded, "Not on my watch!"

An attendant was placing candles in the windows of the Peyton Randolph House. While she was in the library, the door to one of the bookcases swung open. She tried to close it, but it would not budge. She finished her task with the candles and then returned to the library. The door still would not move. She said aloud, "I need to close this bookcase before I leave this room. If there is something you want out of it, please take it and let me close the door." She was immediately able to close the case.

When two guides were closing down the Capitol for the night, one headed to the break room in the basement for her belongings. She didn't bother to turn on the lights. Walking downstairs, she heard someone whistling in the basement. As she realized that her colleague was upstairs and no one else was in the building, the whistling stopped. Spooked, she dashed into the room to grab her belongings and ran directly into the table. She started to scream. Her colleague hurried to her. He told her: "When it comes to ghosts, if you ignore them, they'll ignore you." He said that when he first started working in the building, he had had all kinds of strange experiences, like weird sounds and smells.

One day when it was his turn to close the building, he went from room to room and said in each, "I know you are here; from now on, I'm ignoring you." In the fifteen years since, he has never had another run-in with a ghost.

Dr. Goodwin's Gladsome Ghosts

"I wouldn't give a hoot for anybody who doesn't believe in ghosts." So said the Reverend W. A. R. Goodwin, the visionary behind the restoration of Williamsburg. Early in the twentieth century, the rector of Bruton Parish Church had the dream of restoring Williamsburg to its former glory. In 1926 he persuaded John D. Rockefeller Jr. to fund the project. Together the two planned to re-create and interpret the colonial and Revolutionary life of the town. "Shut your eyes and see the gladsome ghosts who once made these places their home," Goodwin once said. The same year, Bruton Parish acquired the George Wythe House for the rector to use as the parish house for his family. The Wythe House is thought to be one of the most haunted in Williamsburg. Three ghosts in particular frequent the house. Goodwin said of them, "They are very elusive ghosts and refuse to be delineated or described within the limits of any paragraph that might be written. The only way to come to know these spirits is to come here and hold communion with them." Perhaps Goodwin was joking, or perhaps he was referring to the hundreds of years of history living in the buildings and on the streets of this hallowed town. Or perhaps not. . . .